LEADERSHIP THROUGH LOVE

*Both Are Needed
In Order To Properly
Administrate & Appreciate
Those Who Serve Together
in His Kingdom*

Steve Martin

Copyright © 2014 by Steve Martin

LEADERSHIP THROUGH LOVE
Both Are Needed In Order To Properly Administrate & Appreciate Those Who Serve Together in His Kingdom
By Steve Martin

ISBN-13: 978-1495330735

Printed in the United States of America

All rights reserved solely by the author. The author guarantees all contents are original and do not infringe upon the legal rights of any other person or work. No part of this book may be reproduced in any form without the permission of the author.

The views expressed in this book are solely those of the author and publisher, Martin Lighthouse Publishing.

A special thanks to Karla Shrake, who helped edit Chapter 3 on women in the church/ministry and marketplace. Thanks Karla!

Front and back cover design by
Ben Martin
Possible Web Marketing

Dedication

Every person serving with a ministry, church, business or in the home has gifts from the Lord to use in that service. If we understand what our gifts are, we can best contribute in the needed work.

I dedicate this book to each of you who are giving yourself in love for His purposes. In this you will find fulfillment and joy, as you serve your fellow man. This indeed pleases our Lord.

Endorsements

In a rough and tumble world marred by the superficial and the phony, where nothing can be counted on, Steve Martin maps out a straight-line path for Christian organizations. In reality, it's a book on how to steward the factors that too often get side-tracked when navigating a significant call of God. It's a down-to-earth manual of wisdom needed to enable Christian organizations to keep their eye on the big picture, while building a firm foundation to enable it to happen. Steve writes from the stance of one who has served in key administrative roles in a number of key ministries. Every ministry head and administrator will profit from this straight forward operating wisdom.

Morris Ruddick
Entrepreneur, Author, Minister, Consultant and Business Coach

What a great practical book for administration. I have watched Steve oversee several ministries. I know of no better administrator than my friend, Steve Martin. I highly recommend that you read this book.

Dr. Peter Wyns, President, Christians for Messiah Ministries and Pastor of Antioch International Church. Dr. Wyns is also the grandson of Derek Prince.

God has created in Steve a heart for worship and service. His desire has been to see the body of Christ united and to see ministries come together to co-labor for the purposes of God.

Jack Alongi, former Director of Development at Derek Prince Ministries

I had the pleasure of working on an almost daily basis with Steve Martin for many years while he served several Christian ministries. While Steve had the control of whether we worked together, he always made me feel we were working as a team with a common reward in serving God. He enjoyed my family as I did his. He is intelligent, thoughtful, patient to the extent he could be, a good listener, open to new ideas, joyful and passionate about serving the Lord. The projects may be over long ago but not the bond we hold to this day.

George Payne Write Hand Publishing Andalusia, Alabama

We are honored to write an endorsement. Anyone that has worked with you Steve knows what a blessing you are and I was SO HAPPY to read that you finally realize the gifting that God has given you. Love to Laurie and the family.

Jeanette Alongi, formerly of Derek Prince Ministries - Fort Lauderdale, FL and Charlotte, NC

I just finished reading Steve Martin's new book, "Leadership Through Love" - Steve's heart of goodness and faithfulness to His God shines on every page. Of great importance is the practical hands-on wisdom that comes from actually leading through love, giving integrity to the words that are written. Steve's sense of humor always kind of sneaks up on me, and I found myself chuckling so many times at his stories and honest, from-the-heart insights! It is the mandate of all of us who follow the One called Faithful and True to complete the work that our Father has given us, and Steve's book will shine the light on how to do just that, whether you are an administrator or leader in the secular marketplace or in volunteer or paid ministry positions. Loving leadership – a high calling – Steve's done it, and it shows in this book!

Cathy Hargett, Founder/Director, Highway to Zion Ministries

Steve - I read your excellent book! I want to share this: I've known Steve now for several years. He's a man of faith and a man of action! Both are desired in true men of God. Steve is a manager - management is something he knows and can help you with. His future may be in ever-expanding ways, but he can help you manage. Read this book intently - honor the Lord by letting it wash over you and help you become the Manager that God intends you to be. And Steve, thanks for the book - thanks for your honesty and openness! Amen and blessing!

Robbie Phillips, Founder, Present Word Ministries - Columbia, SC

Steve, I finished your book "Leadership through Love". I think it is a great book, one that will help those who choose to glean from your practical (tried and proven) pointers, and at the same time, woven through the pages are thoughts and encouragements to those reading it, to build a good biblical foundation from which to lead and serve from.

I had the pleasure and great blessing of serving under the leadership of Steve Martin for five years. I witnessed firsthand his integrity and faithfulness. I watched him lead me and others with respect, appreciation, love and boundless encouragement. Although our paths have taken other directions over the past six years, I cherish his friendship which continues on today. I nicknamed Steve, "Heavy Hand of Blessings" because I have never met a person who takes such pure delight in blessing others as Steve Martin. I was blessed to call him Boss and am continually blessed to call him friend.

Terri Whitaker, Derek Prince Ministries

Every now and then you have the privilege to get to know someone whose character and life radiate honesty, sincerity, loyalty and Christian love. Steve Martin is that type of person. I first met Steve at a Messianic conference in Charlotte, NC, in 2007. One of the things I quickly noticed about Steve was how "approachable" he was. Even though he was the US Director of an international ministry, he still had time to talk with people at the conference and demonstrated a genuine interest in helping to bring about a network of Believers, as well as area groups and churches, for the purpose of serving the Lord more effectively. As the years have passed I've come to realize just how deep Steve's roots of love and service for the Lord are.

It has been exciting to walk with Steve, as he's "stepped out of the boat" and moved ahead with the vision the Lord gave him for LOVE FOR HIS PEOPLE - a ministry that helps connect Believers around the world with the people of Israel. He is a husband, father and grandfather. Steve, and his wife Laurie, serve as leaders of the Ahava Love Band, a group of singers and musicians who provide praise and worship at area assemblies. Whether you call him Messianic, a part of the "one new man", or a "Jewish Rooter", if there's anyone who knows how to demonstrate "Leadership Through Love", it's Steve Martin.

Curtis Loftin Founder, Beit Yeshua Lincolnton, NC

Thanks for the opportunity to read and review this book. I enjoyed it and thought it had some really great insights. I wish I had this back in my "corporate" days. You are a good writer too. In a world filled with an ever increasing list of 'how to' books, Steve Martin has provided one which clearly sets itself apart from the rest. He presents a concise look at the art/science of management and leadership based not on academia but on real life experiences founded on God's Word and powered by the Holy Spirit. Based on his vast personal experiences in leadership, reinforced by insights received from others, Steve provides truly practical instruction in how to lead and manage an effective organization whether it consists of one or one thousand people. If you are a manager, leader, or hope to one day become one, this book is a must read.

Dr. Richard E. Tompkins, President, Explore Truth Ministries

Steve Martin has a gift from God. He is a visionary. That cannot be taught and few people have that. I've worked with him for three ministries. I was always amazed at how he could take a company from being in the red financially and turn it around into the black - sometimes in a short period of time. I used to say "You should write a book and workbook too." As his friend for over 24 years, I know anyone who reads this book will say "Wow!" too and gain much timely wisdom.

Indira Persad, Founder, Indira Persad Ministries Charlotte, NC

I worked with Steve for five years, assisting him in photography in one of the ministries. It was an honor to work alongside of him. He made the job so much fun. The Steve that I got to know did everything that he has written about in his book, "Leadership Through Love". This is a must read book for anyone who is struggling in their administrative jobs. It will help you to re-focus on what really matters.

Sandra McCain, Fort Mill, SC

After a few years of living in a wheelchair, the day came when the Lord revealed Himself to me. And while I sat in that wheelchair He spoke to me and said, *"Lech Lecha! Go to Jerusalem and pray for the peace and love for My city!"* After my return He made me walk again and started to use me as a pastor of a Messianic Jewish congregation. And with that congregation we started to support a humanitarian work named Vision for Israel & The Joseph Storehouse in Israel. Then several years ago Steve Martin and I met each other for the first time in Israel while serving for this same humanitarian organization. He was one of the inspiring members of the organizing team of the Succot Celebration in Jerusalem. My wife Carla and I were impressed about the way this team was working together.

The teamwork was based on love and respect for each other. Since then we met annually in Jerusalem for the Succot Celebration, and every time again it was Steve Martin who showed us in practice that love was the ideal basic in working together and serving people. James says: *"Faith without works is dead!"* The works he means are the works of love. The love we put into our work, in our relations and in all of our life should be the love that God gives us by His Spirit. If we believe, we should use this love; otherwise our faith is nothing. This same love is the theme of this book.

It shows you that the Love of God through each and every one of us should be used as the main part of our work together. Steve is a man who knows this and showed it to us in practice. And he knows how to explain it, as this book will show you by simply giving you some ideas and tools. Therefore we recommend this book to you. Carefully try to implement these ideas into your relations in your work and daily life. May the Lord bless you, Baruch haShem.

Peter Nissen, Beit Emoenah, The Netherlands

"Leadership Through Love" comes from the heart of a man who has been there; who has managed, administrated and served for several decades and he is one who has indeed done it not only excellently, but also from the motivation of love. His writing reveals the foundational backbone upon which leadership and oversight must rest; love toward God first and secondly love, respect and honor toward the people God has created in His image - our coworkers and staff. And because Steve's foundational motive is right on and rock-solid, the insights, lessons and wisdom-nuggets he offers so eloquently and succinctly are also right on and rock-solid.

While there are volumes of books on the mechanics of administrating and managing, the author has brought forth in "Leadership Through Love" the all-important underlying truth that must be the motivating factor behind it and all its aspects. He speaks to the heart of those who are called to lead and oversee - not for their own personal interests or ambitions, but as those who desire to reflect the heart and nature of their heavenly Father.

He systematically lays out the pragmatic nuts and bolts that are required to manage and oversee in a creative, productive and excellent manner.

Sharing candidly from his own personal journey of experience, he covers some of the pitfalls common to administrating and how they can be avoided – very valuable lessons indeed. For those who aspire to or feel called to roles of leadership administration, this book will be a very valuable tool in not only the mechanics of leadership, but also in the heart of leadership.

On a personal note I have known Steve and Laurie Martin since 1990 and I can testify that they are people of consistent impeccable character and Christ-likeness. They are humble, kind and honoring of others and they have gained great wisdom through the many seasons of walking their faith-journeys. They have endured bitter winter-seasons in suffering deep disappointment, but they have kept their hearts right and have overcome and come forth as purified gold. So dear reader, open wide your heart and receive from this father-of-the-faith as he – and his wife alongside him - have much to teach and share with us. All glory and honor go to our Father in heaven who administrates and oversees all creation and His family of mankind in perfect harmony and love. By His grace, may we learn His ways of "Leadership Through Love."

Karla Shrake, Mantles of Glory Ministries, Dallas, TX

I am pleased to add my personal endorsement to this creative endeavor by Steve Martin. I have had the honor to know Steve for nearly ten years. Steve is a prolific writer, who has a wonderful gift of being able to share his experiences and insights of life in a practical, yet humorous style. His writings are often full of delightful "nuggets of truth" which he has gleaned from his remarkable walk with the Lord these many years.

Dr. William Duerfeldt, Asheville, NC

Reading Steve Martin's new book 'Leadership through Love' led me to a tear and a quick repentance. How often we can overlook the journey for the objective - what we do as opposed to who we are. Steve uses his life testimony to shine light on the importance of loving relationship in the workplace. It is good to be reminded of that, in spite of our great visions. The higher we climb in the Kingdom the greater the responsibility and the more numerous the people we need to serve and love. I thoroughly recommend this book to all in business and ministry. Thank you Steve for reminding me to love the people I work with.

Martin Powell, Kingdom Talents, Owner

Contents

Introduction		Page 13
Chapter 1	A Gift for His Purposes	Page 14
Chapter 2	Use the Tools You Have, But Not the Staff	Page 19
Chapter 3	Women Arising in the Workplace	Page 24
Chapter 4	Train and Let Loose	Page 27
Chapter 5	Burn Candles at Both Ends?	Page 32
Chapter 6	The Visionaries Need You!	Page 36
Chapter 7	Staff Fun Times	Page 40
Chapter 8	It Doesn't All Depend On You	Page 42
Chapter 9	Practically Speaking and Walking	Page 47
Chapter 10	Meetings – Need Them?	Page 50
Chapter 11	Acknowledge Him in All Ways	Page 53
Chapter 12	Another Man's Vineyard	Page 57
And Now My Own		Page 61
About the Author		Page 62
Contact Information		Page 64

Introduction

For over 40 years of my life, my job and position in businesses and church/ministries has been given to being the office manager, the manager, the administrator, the Director of Operations & Finance, or the guy who "wore all the hats and got the job done."

Often during those years I wanted to be "the man" at the top, the one who called the shots, steered the ship, or set the policies. Or the one who traveled the road and airways, while others sat behind the desk doing the 40 hours instead of me.

But the Lord has clearly shown me that my role was very vital to those who did those things, and though I longed to do what they did at times, they couldn't have done their job if I wasn't doing mine. I was to do what I had been gifted and called to do.

Where would churches, ministries or businesses be without the administrators, the directors of departments, or the executive secretaries and administrative assistants? Those organizations who have them know their value. Those who don't may or may not realize what they are missing.

It has been my desire to share a bit of what I have experienced, and learned, in those years. Each one of you who now serves in this capacity is very important to the "visionaries". The work that you do, and the support that you consistently give, enables the top leaders of the organization to do what they have been given by the Lord to do. I like to think of our role as similar to that of my Biblical heroes. Joshua was there for Moses and Timothy served with Paul.

May the Lord encourage you as you read my thoughts and what has worked for me. I hope the stories and suggestions will impart to you further measures of blessing, for those you support and also to those you give direction to.

Steve Martin

Chapter 1

A Gift For His Purposes

Growing up in Cedar Falls, Iowa, in the northeast corner of the Hawkeye State, was a destiny that I am most grateful for. This was a good town to continue my youth, after the three farm years in Minnesota, which I remembered little about, there in the Midwest. While being raised by Dad and Mom Martin, along with the seven other kids in the family, back on Main Street, it didn't seem like anything out of the ordinary to do my part of the kitchen duties, household chores, and to obey when told to "do it now or forget watching TV tonight" orders. That was the way I knew the typical life to be in the late '50's and early '60's.

This very training, as a young boy, along with the sense that the Lord was putting something special in my life, as a gift, I believed was to prepare me for what would come later down the road. I thought that destiny was to be a Catholic missionary priest to Africa. Forty years later though, it had resulted in more than twenty years of Christian ministry, not as the typical minister, but as an "add-ministry", or better known to many, an administrator.

Being the second child in the family, the first son of three, mixed among five daughters, gave me many opportunities to learn some basic instructions in life, which then was used to bring growth to this gift the Lord had placed within me.

As what I knew to be "normal" in large families at that time, I was called upon to take my turn in the nightly kitchen supper cleanup, as my sisters Sue and Mary and I rotated the regular chores after the dinner hour. For so it was always somehow written, on the wall calendar every day of the month, each of our names, listing who was to pick up the table and sweep the floor, who was to wash the dishes, and who was to dry and put away the cleaned pots, pans, silverware, cups, plates, and whatever else was used in service that night. Never mind about these "kitchen duties" being the work of the females – do it or forget about getting my weekly allowance of $0.50.

And so from the third grade until the eighth grade, I diligently labored in the Martin household kitchen, after we had eaten our family meal together. It was generally around 5 pm, on the dot, that we all sat down to eat. Dad would get home from his first job at 4:30 pm, from the local Viking Pump Foundry, and then, right after supper, was off to his "2nd job". This personal business was called Martin Electrical Services, his own proprietorship of wiring houses and other electrical service jobs for the people of Cedar Falls, Iowa. Feeding this family of ten took more than the regular 40 hour job, even with the additional ten hours of overtime each week he was allowed to do at Viking.

Early in my high school years I would earn some extra cash helping him, but after a while pulling on the white and black wires through the plaster and slat walls, and climbing around blown-in insulation above ceilings, wasn't my idea of the "good life".

In between the kitchen chores and the electrical apprenticeship, I was able to secure the Waterloo Courier newspaper route, just a few bike blocks from our house to the trailer court. I started with less than 30 trailers to deliver to, but after a few contests put on by the newspaper print company, once earning myself a portable cassette player (a big deal to me in 1968!) and other items too expensive to purchase on my own, the route grew to 62 Sunday deliveries, along with the daily delivery increase. Getting the afternoon paper to their door before they got home from work, and then making the collections on the weekends or after school for payment, kept me on the move.

Tracking down the bi-weekly collections, sometimes meaning two to three trips biking on my Schwinn bike, totally equipped with baskets over the rear wheel, to those "delinquent" customers to see if they were home, not only increased my leg power for the three years of middle school football and track teams, but it also increased the persistence necessary to make sure I got my money the people owed me. If I didn't, so went my profit. When people moved out on me, and owed for a month or more, my appreciation for those who paid on time and didn't allow their debt to grow became a strong motivator to have that attribute in my own life. As for the debtors, hopefully they repented of their wayward ways, and never did it to the next guy.

I also did my turn at Rolinger's Restaurant, as one of the male waiters in the all-male employees local food establishment. Being able to give the cooks, the older boys typically in the high school senior class, a good, readable chicken and fries order, was very important. Or delivering the customer order having the cheeseburger basket, along with the orange shake, which was the hope of the owner to make him rich and famous. It didn't.

Russ Rolinger, co-owner with his father Lou, the ex-boxer, seemed to always complain that McDonald's stole his "Hi-Boy" idea and just re-named it the Big Mac. All in all, I grew in knowledge about further getting things done on time. "Hot food first" was the daily command from both Russ and Lou.

After a few years at this after-school and weekend job, I too became a veteran, and was able to start training the younger ones, who were just turning thirteen years of age, and freshmen in high school. The gift of management within was being groomed for the long haul.

When the $1.10 hourly rate in the restaurant business didn't quite make the extra spending money that I wanted, or felt that I really needed, my job search took me to the Eagle grocery store in my senior year of high school. I had to quit the Columbus High School Sailors football team that I was on though, the very week before we were to play my home town team of Cedar Falls High School. But because I was at the Catholic high across town in Waterloo, I didn't know any of the Tiger football players anyway, so the new job took higher priority. Sitting on the bench, my number 88 stuck between numbers 87 and 89 among the others who didn't play much, helped convince me that football wasn't the way I was going anyway.

Sports had been good to me, especially baseball. In my junior year, our spring baseball team made it to the state finals, losing 1-0 to the state champs from Mason City. It had been a good year – I set the team school record in triples and walks, playing center field most of the time. During a game my senior year, I played every position, after asking my coach Duke Dutkowski to let me have a shot at it.

When graduation finally arrived in the spring of 1973, after being at the grocery store for less than a year, the night stock manager of the Eagles store asked me if I was interested in taking over the crew. He had seen "something in me" that both he and the general store manager, Phil Bailey, liked. I guess I pulled the pallets out in good order each night, and stocked a pretty good grocery aisle that caught their attention. Or maybe it was the "singing along with the night time radio DJ as loud as I could" energy, when things seemed a bit too quiet, that appealed to their observations. (But I doubt that. To this day, I tend to sing louder than most!)

Not wanting to live like a screech owl, coming out only at night, I graciously, but thankfully, declined the offer, and went instead a year later to work at the local Sartori Hospital in Cedar Falls as a daytime custodian. Scrubbing the scum away from the hallway floor baseboards and the cigarette-smoke buildup on the patient's rooms ceiling grid lasted less than a year, but building diligence and character, no matter what the job entailed, would prove beneficial as the future positions opened before me. And it was a neat time hanging with the University of Northern Iowa football player, the team's star running back, my co-worker, during his off-season.

Along the way there were those I watched and learned from. Everyone needs another one or two to show them the ropes. Usually it was the big brother of a friend, since I didn't have a big brother of my own. Or the guy who had six months more experience doing what I was being trained to do at the time. Whatever the case, it seemed like a good thing to watch and see how a task was accomplished, and then try to find a quicker way of doing it myself. Time has always been a top priority to me. (The clocks around my home, office, and history room will attest to that!) A step here or there would cut down on the physical load, and make the task get completed quicker than when others would do the same thing.

Since I always had the feeling that another was watching me, as was most often the case at home with my seven siblings, I always felt I needed to set a good example. And then I wouldn't have to confess the sin of "setting a bad example" in the weekly confessional. This sense of responsibility started at a young age, and has been with me ever since.

When I was in the eighth grade, I was given the opportunity to schedule the altar boys for the weekday, special events and Sunday Masses. I suppose Father Purtell saw that I paid attention in his catechism class, and thus asked me if I would do the task. It didn't take too long to do a two-month schedule for each of the five Sunday Masses, but when it came time to do the funerals, which couldn't be "booked" until the week before the event, not knowing when those were coming, proved a bit tougher. When I couldn't find two sixth, seventh or eighth grade boys to serve Mass, I usually ended up doing it myself. (Not a good way to learn delegating!)

But as all things seemed to even out, when it came time to schedule the altar boys for the weddings, I most certainly scheduled myself as often as I could. For it just so happened that most of the bridegrooms, being happy as they were on their special occasion, would generally slip me a five dollar bill before departing in their decorated wedding car. And the Lord blessed me with many weddings at St. Patrick's church!

Making the best of the way things were, by doing that which I was being taught to do, continued to add to the natural and spiritual character being built within. Though always smaller in stature than my classmates around me, the Lord was using the natural training and instruction to build a "bigger" stature, which those on the outside didn't always see.

He was preparing me for His greater purposes for the road ahead.

Chapter 2

Use the
Tools, Not the Staff

-Do unto them as you would…
-Treasure the people, while digging the foundations
-Bless and curse not - honor those who serve with you

After my high school days in Iowa, the Lord had me spend a year at the University of Northern Iowa, before moving to LaSalle-Peru, Illinois in the summer of 1976. I was supposed to have received a transfer through the Eagles food chain, but when I arrived on the scene, no such position was available. They hadn't even heard of me, as my previous manager had told me they would.

And so I got a job at a local restaurant, the English Muffin, alongside my brother-in-law David Johnson, and sister Mary, who had both moved to this town a few years earlier. Soon an assistant manager position opened at the Kerr-McGee lumber yard, which I promptly took, since I was now engaged to my fiancée Laurie Unzicker, and needed to prepare for the days to come.

Working alongside three friends in the office and the yard continued to show me the importance of appreciating those you labor with. You get close to each other when you share common goals on the job, and entrust yourselves to the other one to complete the task.

The yard manager, George Rhodes, and I, needed to build a new pole barn to house the steel siding we were adding to the inventory, so after the poles were put in place by the Plow Creek construction crew, a common purse Christian community at a nearby farm setting, George and I put the 18' sheets of metal together. Fighting the wind at times, we entrusted ourselves to the other one, so the metal wouldn't cut into our hands as we held it in place, to be nailed into the 2" x 6" side boards.

With Kevin Grafton and our other member of the crew, Kelly Hass, supplying the parts and holding steady the tractor platform on which we nailed from, we learned the importance of each one respecting the part the other fulfilled. Teamwork was always important, as I learned on the playing field, and now on the job.

The Lord Jesus Himself gave us valuable lessons, while He led His band of men and women on earthly team, which has proven itself to be most applicable in my leading of business and ministry staffs. These very effective truths in administrating were spoken by Him, when He said to His small band, "Do unto others as you would have them do unto you" and "You shall love your neighbor as yourself." (Matthew 22:39)

These were two of my key attitudes I took early on in my management positions, as I learned how to be a "manager of the people", as one other executive team member put it, during one of my years with Derek Prince Ministries (1987-1990 and 2001-2005).

Not wanting to be one who "lords it over others", demanding my own way and using the "staff rather the tools", I took the posture of treating the staff who served with me as I desired my boss to treat me - honoring them as I wanted to be recognized and honored, and uplifting them as I often needed, but rarely received, in some cases. As I sought to encourage each one in my care, even as a pastor does his flock, I found that the love grew between them and I. When those bonds were established, staff readily would give beyond the call of duty and pay, as they knew my heart was not just for the job to be done, but for them in helping me get it done.

Not only did we labor together for the cause of the Lord in the ministry, with me as the recognized leader and their boss, but we became friends for the long haul. I still treasure and continue to keep relationships with those who were in the same office setting with me, or on the church volunteer teams, as fellow servants. Taking a heart position of being their servant, and not one seeking to be served, created and maintained unique, precious, and long term relationships.

Because of friendships I established with my employees, there were occasions when I had to cut staff, and even terminate some. Because of the respect I still had for them, and with them knowing my heart for them even after their termination, did not mean the "end-of-the-line" in our friendship. I still maintain communication with ones that were let go from my staff. Though the tasks and the outworking of those tasks may not have been performed to expectations and ministry office needs, they still knew that I respected them as a person. They knew that my desire was to see them move on and find a better setting for their skills and lives. Rejection was not going to follow them out the door. They still had dignity and appreciation for the time we served together.

Far too often when people were asked to leave a staff position, it was assumed, and sometimes even expected, that the relationship that was created on the job left with them, once they were no longer part of the business or ministry staff. That should not happen, and rarely happened when people left staff I supervised. I didn't want bridges burned when the Lord moved me on, and so I didn't burn the bridge when others left the staff.

Even when it came to volunteers, the many who gave of themselves for weekends at the forty-three conferences I administrated, enjoyed coming back when I called on them each time. They knew they were appreciated and valued, not just for the time and energy they always gave, but for the gift of themselves that they freely gave.

Several staff members from one ministry or business that we worked together at providentially wound up on my office team again, some in another city and location than our previous time together. With one, it was after nine years had passed without seeing each other except once or twice.

In another case, there were twenty six years of time between our years of having a job together, and then other jobs apart, in other states. So it was with my good friend and best man at our wedding thirty years prior, Kevin Grafton. Kevin and I worked together at the Kerr-McGee wholesale lumber yard in Mendota, Illinois for three years, from 1977-1980, and then, because we kept the bond of friendship alive, even as my family moved to three different states over the next twenty five years, we again joined arm in arm in 2004 for the work of the humanitarian aid center of Vision For Israel, in Charlotte, NC. Even though I was again his "boss", due to the different service areas we were given to do, the approach we both took was to respect the position the other had, and continue our friendship on and off the clock.

Another attitude I try to apply, I will word as "treasure the people, while digging the foundation." Involved with businesses and ministries that I was employed at, some at the foundational stages of their work, I found that it is so important to show appreciation for those who work with you. Even while being in a "boss-employee" relationship, showing people are valued first for who they are, and then for what they do, will benefit the administration of the tasks being given and completed.

No building foundation is built without digging "below the surface", and as you build a relationship of caring and encouraging your staff, they will see the concern you have for them. Going beyond the surface level on the job relationships will bring strength when tough times come, and you further need to depend on your staff to help get you through those tasks.

One way I enjoyed showing appreciation and honor for my staff was to bless them on their birthday, which gave them a special day that was especially for them. Cake, ice cream, even balloons and other birthday specialties showed my love for them, and desire to honor them, with them being in the spotlight. People know you really do care when you express appreciation for them in ways that show you took some time and effort to bring it about.

Take opportunities like this to also share with the rest of the staff something about your department member, if that is the case, that would uplift them in their peers' presence. I found that sharing a Bible verse, which exemplifies a character aspect they have, not only encourages the individual, but the others who hear it, to press on even more in that area of appreciation.

As so often seems to be the case, the boss or leader of the group gets the recognition when a major task is completed, leaving the rest of the team sometimes wondering why the glory wasn't shared across-the-board. Making a staff member the spotlight on these special days, and speaking not only words of joy but also giving of thanks for them, will go a long way in both task production and loyalty.

Another way to express thanks for personal staff contributions can come by taking the time to go to lunch one-on-one. This gives them the space to share things that may not be expressed in the hectic business hours. Some time away from the office setting, even for a lunch period if possible, gives the employee an opportunity to discuss feelings and concerns that are not as easy with the boss sitting behind his or her desk.

Learning to bless and not curse those who labor with you, under your oversight, will actually give you more "tools" to enable your staff to grow. People will know you are not using them for the "tools" they are, but that they are being allowed to grow and prosper for their benefit also. Knowing that they themselves are the treasures, having talents and gifts to share in the work at hand, will get the foundation and the building built that you are administrating in a strong and enduring fashion.

Chapter 3

Women Arising in the Marketplace

-All are created – make the most of this!
-If the Shoe Fits, Have Them Wear It

In today's business and ministry world, women have entered the work force in record numbers. While it has become the norm in recent decades that women desire to work outside the home, many have been forced to because of financial pressures on the family budget. In addition there are many single Moms that have to be the sole support of their children. (Another book could be written on this alone, and "what happened to the men!")

There are many women available in the workforce who carry the gifts, the heart, and the ability to perform well in all arenas of business, church and ministry staffs. My encouragement and exhortation to men in positions of hiring and management authority is to find the best person for the job, regardless of gender. While women have made progress in having more and more opportunities for the higher level jobs, there can still be obstacles of old ways of thinking from the past.

Let's recognize that gifted women supervisors can very effectively steer those in their charge, with skill, attitude, and favor. And when they do they need to be paid with the same benefits that a man would be, if having that same authority and responsibility.

While employed as the Director of Operations and Finance at Derek Prince Ministries, we had two women supervisors, Jeanette Alongi, Communications Supervisor, and Gina Stasko, Customer Service Supervisor. When they spoke at our weekly managers' team meetings I gave full attention to their excellent input, wisdom and knowledge in overseeing their department staff, which was a combination of both men and women.

I respected and was impacted by the administrative leadership of both Jeanette Alongi (who had more than 24 years with the ministry at the time of her retirement) and Gina Stasko (almost 25 years at the time of this writing). So many times they gave thought provoking opinions, great suggestions and encouraging support that enabled the ministry to advance forward.

Another woman that I held high regard for, having much godly character, and whom I admired with deep respect and honor, was the Finance Supervisor and personal secretary of Derek Prince, Dorothy Schulte. It was Dorothy who spent the time training me, when I first came on staff with Derek Prince Ministries in 1987 to replace her, as she came to the end of her faithful years of dedicated service before her retirement year.

Dorothy would hold me to strict accounting practices, to the very penny when balancing the books, and would not let me "cut corners" to save time, at any time. Her commitment and loyalty to her work certainly helped give the ministry the creditability that it has long held, in part to her supervision, and which I strove to carry on in my tenure. She was indeed the "woman for the job".

As I looked to fill positions, both due to expansion and turnover, I regularly interviewed both men and women whom I would then select to be the one for that needed addition. And as it was in my authority, I worked to pay them the same for the work performed, whether they were a man or a woman performing that work. In my eyes, as I looked to the Lord, each are created equally, and are to be treated equally. If the shoe fits, men, let the woman wear it!

As a result of having several leadership positions with businesses and ministries, in the administrator and higher management roles, I have gained the respect of other leaders, in other businesses and ministries, who have come to value my opinion and input. Thus, when it was asked of me who I would recommend for a leading ministry position for a work located in Jerusalem, it did not take me long to put forward the name of Hannele Pardain, who at the time of this writing continues to be the Christian Friends of Israel USA Director. Hannele has led this ministry very much so with her diligence, long hours and heart for the people and land of Israel. I wholeheartedly recommended her for this vital leadership position that was needed to be filled at that time.

Women in leadership can have a more nurturing heart than can sometimes be typically found in men. (And sometimes not!) They may not be as quick to reprimand someone in their department, realizing more of the factors involved in the decision having to be made. I have found that they are more longsuffering when it comes to choosing a course that would take more patience, than a man in that position would take. Often it turns out to be the right course as more details are later known in the situation - it must be the "mother instinct" that always believes the best about her child!

On several occasions I had been told that I am too "black and white" in my memo and e-mail communications. One of the best administrative assistants that I have ever had, Charlotte Mytrysak, during my time with DPM, would often encourage me to use "more honey" in my expressions, both in writing memos and speaking to staff. I tend to want to get to the point, tell it like it is (as I see it) and get the matter settled. Her important input was to let me know that this can still be done, but with a little less "pepper" and "more honey" in my approach. The results proved that her observation was accurate – so again, the woman's touch and discernment can be most beneficial.

May the Lord continue to give us more women who have the time, the heart, and the skills to take their place in His work. *And may male leadership step into this new day by recognizing, welcoming, and celebrating these women!*

Chapter 4

Train and Let Loose

-It Is Who You Know
-Hire To Complement Your Strengths
  - where, not if, you are weak, then let them be strong
-Outsource as needed

People come and people go. So much of the USA is on the move, shifting here and there. No wonder residential real estate firms continue to do well most of the time, as people change jobs, and often need to re-locate within cities, or to other cities.

When my father, Louis Martin, retired from the Viking Pump Company, he had been there for over 30 years. When our family lived at 1116 Main Street in Cedar Falls, Iowa, I had been in that same home from 1st grade until my first (and only) year in college. My wife's parents lived in the same house for 48 years, in Peru, Illinois. As of 2014, Lorraine still does, even after Otto's passing on to his eternal glory with his Lord and Savior Jesus.

It is more common these days for people to move from house to house, city to city, state to state, as jobs change, due to transitions with companies themselves, and with the employees. How do administrators find good people to meet the business, church or ministry needs, as they themselves grow, or fluctuate with life around them?

Often it is said that it is not "what you know but who you know." And I would agree, based on my understanding of relationships, and the years of experience which has proved this to be so in my hiring selections.

Personality tests abound, resumes are plentiful, but I have yet to be convinced that what is "tested" in a twenty minute survey or written by a potential candidate in a resume' is as trustworthy as knowing people themselves. And how do you get to know people that can do what you need done on the job? The Holy Spirit is my guide. He has promised to lead me and direct my steps. I believe that holds true when it comes time for an administrator or human services director to make the changes necessary within the staffing positions. Out of relationships within the church, or through networking with other ministries and businesses, we can get to know people who have the skills required, or can be trained to do the tasks needed.

My first goal as the one doing the hiring is to know the person's character, which weighs more heavily in my book than even their skill level. If I see someone who is trustworthy, diligent, having a servant's heart and attitude, and teachable, I am far better ahead bringing them on staff, than going out and selecting someone who I have no history of involvement with. I have found that selecting someone with the character within, who has the willingness and the spirit to be taught that which they may not know as yet, will better serve the organization, and will learn the tasks that the work requires.

One who "knows it all" brings a pride and attitude with them that has proven detrimental when placed on your team in the workplace. Those not willing to cooperate, receive instructions, and "hear and obey" your leadership will only bring trouble down the road. Careful observance beforehand will save a lot of headache later.

Once a new employee is trained sufficiently to do the regular routines, let them have enough space to create better ways of doing them. Freedom to grow, by not being controlled by the boss, will cause the employee to make it their own, or take ownership, as my good friend Jack Alongi so often said, at Derek Prince Ministries.

We had one employee, a young man with no leadership skills initially, that came to work before my time at one ministry. He started out in the shipping department, doing the mail runs, filling book and cassette orders, and basically doing what he was told to do. At times though he had disagreements with his supervisor, and on one occasion, after she and I concurred on what to do, we gave him a day off with no pay, over an incident that required noticeable action. This drove home our point.

As the years went by, his supervisor, Liz Spooner, (another employee who had worked 25 years on the job!) retired, and because he had put himself "under the rule" to be taught, we gave him the staff position of being the Shipping Supervisor. Today, Brian Kelson has his own web design business, and has grown into a very fine man. His character allowed him to mature, and his teachable spirit gave him the means to learn the job, and become that which his mentors had taught him over the years.

The Lord has given each of us gifts. Encouraging your staff to take something, and expand it, brings fulfillment to them, and will "profit" the organization more. Controlling every situation, such as micro-managers do, only stifles the atmosphere and the office members.

Once certain boundaries have been put in place, for the Lord is a God of order and not chaos, then let the staff member operate out of his or her ability to think, respond, and implement new ideas and ways to complete the task. Even accounting, which I myself learned on the job, has standard operating procedures, but there is always more than one way "to skin a cat."

Boredom caused by mundane routine produces wasted man hours. Let the people have some freedom in their positions, and offer new ideas for consideration. Reward them when their new ideas are put into practice.

Another practice I have found very beneficial in my hiring methods is to look for people who can do those tasks I either cannot do, nor have the time to do. As the leader of the group, you need to have those surrounding you who can complement the team. Face it, you don't have all the answers, nor do you have the time to learn all the answers. But by adding people who are more skilled in areas you are not, and don't even have knowledge about, you make the team stronger, which results in more production.

If someone shows a talent for such a thing as organizing the office supply cabinet, then give them another task that requires even more arrangement of pieces and product in storage. If someone shows a delight in sharing with visitors who come to see the structure of the organization, then make them the "tour guide" for those times.

On the lighter side of the job, as I expressed in a previous chapter, have times to celebrate with the staff a birthday or the completion of a big event, such as a weekend conference. The guy who enjoys cookouts at home can be the "grill master" for the company, and use this joy of cooking to express himself in this manner, while blessing the others.

There are certain jobs that you may not have the skilled personnel or equipment to do what is needed. At these points, outsource to those businesses which are available for such needs. And even as you are doing this, your church or ministry becomes even more known within the community. Scripture speaks of the elder having a good reputation outside the church. Even the director should be spoken highly of in this manner, as he conducts business with those helping him fulfill his tasks for the work.

If a job is one that is only needed for one time, or occasionally, then outsourcing, rather than getting someone trained, is worth the money. Or if the equipment costs prohibit the job from being done internally, then look for a good, reputable company that does this work, and contract the job with them. Employee costs are not only spent for salary, but also insurances, vacations and other benefits. It pays to consider both of these options – hiring or outsourcing.

Bottom line, relationships tend to allow the leader the better choice in finding and keeping good staff members. Allowing staff members to grow in their positions, without the micromanager dictating each task and oversight of it, and outsourcing when needed brings a profitable staff climate in the office.

Chapter 5

Burn Candles at Both Ends? – NOT!

-Rest and Sabbath Days
-Mornings with the Lord
-We all are given 24 hours each day
-Trust in Him at all times

Working seven days a week, 50 or more weeks during the year, is not the Lord's plan for anyone, and certainly not for a church/ministry or business leader. The one who does this will burn out faster than a Roman candle at a July 4th celebration.

Serving with one church/ministry combination for fourteen years proved this in my life. During the continual growth of that ministry, we were staffed with a secretary and myself for a period of four years. After six years in this position, in 1994 we moved the ministry office and three families from Fort Lauderdale, Florida, to Charlotte, North Carolina. In addition to having a family of myself, with my wife Laurie and four children at home (either in grade school, middle or high school), my time was pressed at both ends.

Once having moved to North Carolina, within six months after landing in Charlotte we started building the local church, which took additional time and energy. With annual conferences continuing, starting at two per year and then four, plus Friday all-night prayer meetings from 10 pm until 6 am, followed by Saturday labor in building projects, added to the usual Sunday morning services, the toll indeed took its physical, emotional and spiritual toll on myself and others.

When my father, who had moved here from Iowa in 1997, to help me with the ministry, after his retirement that year (65 years old), died two years later in July, 2000 from lymphoma cancer, my strength and desire to continue on ended soon thereafter. I was burnt out. And when the seemingly only hope and one request I had left, to travel at least once a year on an international ministry trip with the head of the ministry and senior pastor, was not to happen for me, my heart and hope completely left.

I resigned from the church and ministry staff as administrator six months later, and our family left the church in July, 2001. It had just gotten to be too much.

If not for the encouraging prophetic words I had received along the way over the years, and the opportunity to return to Derek Prince Ministries after being gone for ten years, I am not sure where I would have ended up. Nor where my family would have gone. I am not sure it would have been with another ministry. But only because of the Lord, a flicker of hope, still lingering hope in my heart, had not totally gone out. I yet longed to complete the call that had been on my life since my youth.

Early on in my Christian walk, certainly because of the great example my mom, Lila Martin Parker, had set, I still continued to be diligent and faithful with my morning prayer and Bible reading time. Spending the early morning hours with the Lord was not only a good habit, but a necessity, if I was to do what I needed to do in my work of the ministry.

Typically I rise at 4 am and spend the next hour or so reading a chapter from the Bible and then pray in tongues. As I see it, letting the Holy Spirit, Who knows all, pray through me, is more effective than if I personally prayed a list (which is helpful for many though.) As people and thoughts come to my head, in English, I believe that He is taking the direction needed. And so I prayed in tongues often. This is a good practice that I continue to this day. Someday, once I meet my Lord in the heavenly realm, I will certainly begin to know how effective these prayers have been. I do know, as the Scriptures promise, that my inner spiritual being is being built up, and gives me daily strength and wisdom for the responsibilities I maintain.

We each are given 24 hours each day. What we choose to do with them will determine much in the direction we walk, the relationships we have, and the work that is completed. Our daily choices today will determine where we are at next month, next year, and ten years from now.

Back in 1985, as a member of Shiloh Fellowship in East Lansing, Michigan, I heard a message spoken by Erik Krueger, founder and senior pastor of the church (later renamed New Covenant Christian Church), that still speaks to me this day. Erik spoke a word that just sank into my spirit, which I think about on occasion. He simply said that we each are on a path, and along the way there are roads we can take, which will either take us closer to the mark, or farther away from our destiny. Even if we were to take a slight degree shift from our destined path at any point in time, if no course correction later occurred, years down the road we would find ourselves way off course. In some instances, it could be too far off to be corrected, without a major shift or repentance on our part.

We each need the help of others to make sure we continue to walk the walk, and stay on the right road. We need the encouragement of others to see the path ahead, when often it looks like we have come to a cliff, and the only way is down, or to a mountain, and we neither have the strength nor the desire to climb another mountain. (Even if we watch the *Sound of Music* movie many times!)

During the last year of my tenure with All Nations Church and Mahesh Chavda Ministries, when I was struggling to hear the Lord and confirm His direction I felt I needed to take, I called my friend in Andalusia, Alabama, George Payne. George and I first knew each other in the early 1990's, when he had called our Fort Lauderdale office to see if he could print our ministry envelopes. I was fairly blunt at the time, and told him on the phone that we didn't do business with anyone outside of town. Well, the Lord changed that!

Many years later, after using boxes and boxes of envelopes that he had printed, serving together at conferences, and building a long lasting friendship to this day, George was one I could call on for advice. Knowing my situation as well as anyone, he had gained my trust to give me some good counsel. So I called him from my office in Charlotte during the summer of 2000.

He encouraged me to call a lady who had a prophetic gift, whom he had known for years, to ask her if the Lord would give her a word for me. And so I did.

When I called Helen, and introduced myself briefly so as to not give my situation away and let the Lord speak through her, she started praying in tongues, and then shared some very encouraging words. One being that the "changing of the guard was taking place", and that the Lord's direction was to be made clear to me. Truly words of light in my place of darkness and weariness.

The "guard" did change, and my faith was strengthened. Changes were needed, and I gave thanks to the Lord for His rehema word, and His written Word. As I shared above, the Lord had a turn in the road, and within a year I had taken it.

The first Scripture I ever memorized, when I was 18, comes from Psalm 37:4,5, "Have your delight in the Lord, and He will give you the desires of your heart. Trust also in Him, and He will do it." I would be the first to say that I have not always depended on the Lord as I should have, nor did I always trust Him for those daily needs that occurred regularly, but I can testify that I am still walking with Him this day. He has sustained, upheld, protected and watched over me and mine since I first put my trust in Him as a first grader in 1960. The teachers and preachers heard along the way, with the backing of the truth found in the Bible, have kept me on the destiny path the Lord desires.

I have learned not to burn the candles at both ends, to take each Sunday as the holy day of the Lord to rest from my labors, and acknowledge Him in all my ways, along the way. This has been very instrumental in administrating His directives with staff and situations during the building processes.

Chapter 6

The Visionaries Need You!

- They dream it - you make it happen
- It takes a team
- Head Won't Get Far without the Neck
(or heads will roll)

Did you ever see the Headless Horseman movie? The one who rides around in the woods on the horse during the night? (I guess since he can't see, it doesn't matter if it is day or night though, huh?)

Now imagine a head riding around on a horse without a neck, or without the rest of the body. Maybe it could happen in a sci-fi movie, but not in a business or ministry.

Visionaries dream the dreams, speak the dreams, share the dreams, and desire the dreams to come about. But without you, the administrator and the support team (the rest of the body), not much will happen. The Lord has purposely set it in place that His whole Body will be needed for His work to be fulfilled.

You are a very vital part of the work, and without you doing your part, the visionary may not see his or her dream come to fruition. And without you realizing your importance and place in this part of the body, it most likely won't happen. Or at least not to the extent that the Lord knows it can be, and wants it to be.

Without the neck to support the head, which will then allow the head to move about, the head may end up just "rolling around", or being the Headless Horseman riding through the woods, trying to make the dream or vision happen. (Or is this the real picture when we hear or say that the "heads will roll"? A bit comical it is, I think.)

Visionaries need the administrators. They can't "move" without them – in the natural nor in the spiritual.

When I was a younger man, I was with the second ministry that I was blessed to work with, Mahesh Chavda Ministries. Early on in the job as the administrator, I was a bit shaky and lacking much needed confidence. Since 1978, when I first met Mahesh Chavda in LaSalle-Peru, Illinois, I had a real desire to work with this ministry, but after a number of what I thought were "closed doors", it looked like it was not going to happen.

The Lord had been the One who opened this door, in a very clear way earlier, but the right timing had to come to pass, and both sides involved needed to have confirming words that this was indeed the Lord. Unknown to me at the beginning, I would serve with this ministry team for 14 years. A good foundational building for the long term needed to be established, and it was important that we each realized this, as much as we were capable of knowing it.

We see in part, and know in part. So often the Lord needs to give us confirming words of encouragement along the way, to help us keep going, and do what is necessary to keep building the spiritual building.

Two prophetic words were spoken to me, one prior to my coming on staff with MCM, and one during the initial years. The first one occurred during the summer of 1990, in Kansas City, where I had gone with my family to assist Mahesh Chavda at a conference, while on our vacation. Nine months earlier I was supposed to have started with Mahesh Chavda Ministries, but what looked like a "death blow" to the connection had taken place, leaving me almost without a job either at Derek Prince Ministries or MCM. My family and I were thus preparing to move from Fort Lauderdale back to either the Midwest, in the land where Laurie and I grew up, or to Charlotte, NC, where things seemed to be happening spiritually.

At the end of the conference where we were at in Kansas City, I had gone up to the platform to help "catch" those who were "slain in the Spirit" during the prayer time. James Goll, one of the leaders and speakers of the host Kansas City Fellowship, and having a well-known prophetic ministry, came over to me at the end of the prayer time, and spoke this very encouraging word, which put faith back into my heart.

"You are the very one whom this minister needs, to do that which the Lord wants to have done through him. There is not another at this time. It is you whom he needs as the administrator. You have what he needs. You are the man, not another."

Five months later the Lord's time came to pass for me to come on full time on the team of Mahesh and Bonnie Chavda, as the administrator. But during that long five months (and even during the times of doubt that still came later), I made it a point to re-read this prophetic word that had kept me hoping and waiting for the right time to come.

Another encouraging word was spoken to me within the first year in this position. Wanting to do the best I could, with my heart desiring to see Africa, Israel, and the other nations touched that this ministry had an effect in, I had concerns that I still didn't have what was needed for the job. With only one year of college, no degree, and other "lacks" and skills that the world says you need to be an administrator, the concerns seemed understandable and justified.

Bonnie, who I considered my pastor in certain aspects, believing she understood many things I was going through in trying to serve properly, spoke a word to me "out of the blue". As I was doing yard work around their home, as part of my duties, she came up to me and said that my administrative skills weren't just something I had learned in the natural, but was indeed a spiritual gift that the Lord had given me. I had a gift from the Lord, which was in administration. (The Scriptures call it the "gift of helps" as one description.)

That was the first time I had ever heard that. I thought the administrative skills, knowledge and wisdom that I had were strictly due to my upbringing, which certainly had its important part, or the "learning on-the-job" that I had received in my prior fifteen years of management.

What this did was reveal to me that the Lord had placed me in this spiritual position. It was His gifts given to me, for His purposes to be fulfilled, that enabled me to do the job that needed to be done. My lack of natural training was "overlooked" because His Holy Spirit, working in and through me, gave me wisdom and understanding to support the visionary and the ministry.

What I came to understand even more, as the Holy Spirit continued to bring understanding to this gift in my life, was that this gift is one of the foundational stones necessary to build a strong building, and support the work placed upon it. He continued to show me the need that exists within the body of Christ, requiring this gifting, and even more specifically, those who are called to be the visionaries and whom serve in the apostolic work, need this gifting.

The head needs the neck to rest on, move about with, and be a connector to the rest of the body in the church, or the business staff.

The visionaries need you, the administrative team!

Chapter 7

Staff Fun Times - Enjoying Staff Events

- Staff Retreats
- Party Time!
- Birthdays and BBQs
- After Hours

Staffs are often called upon to make events happen, such as the church picnic, the business expo, or the ministry conference. That is part of the job requirements, and understood by all. But serving others makes one desire, and need, a break once in a while, to just relax and "hang out". Just as in families, once a big event has come and gone, the staff needs some down time, apart from the regular job tasks, to enjoy one another and continue to build good relationships. Coming from a large family, I appreciate the opportunities we had, and have, to be with one another, where one is not expected to have to "perform".

Being one who enjoys having a good time, and wanting to see others involved as much as they desire, I saw to it that each staff I was blessed with had times of being together apart from the daily routine or the big event. I realized the importance of having a down time, when the pressures of the daily work or weekend schedule for church weren't pushing hard.

For the monthly birthdays, we made it a point to celebrate these special days in the life of the accountant, the shipping supervisor, the custodian, the editor, or the receptionist. Having all the employees gather in the lunch room, my assistant and I had a birthday cake, ice cream, and sometimes balloons and other decorations ready to bless those whose birthday it was that month. This makes each individual know that they are indeed special and important, and not just someone sitting in the chair getting the job done.

Once a year, we would try to schedule a staff retreat, out of town, for two days and nights. Usually this was after the annual conference, or some other event that had required extra effort and time. Going to a mountain retreat lodge, or a resort where all the food and recreation coordination was done by someone other than our own, was always a much appreciated time together.

Being able to gather after office hours, on a weekend or weekday night, gives employees the chance to appreciate each one even more, with an evening baseball or basketball game, racing event at the track, or a good band playing at the food gathering. Whether the expense is covered by the business, church or ministry, or each pays separately, the staff sees this extra care shown by the key staff and leaders that the whole person is important, in addition to being the one on staff who gets the job done. It is interesting to hear what people say and do when "not on the job". It can be a very positive addition to the ongoing relationships that are important to maintaining good relationships in the office.

Another bonding time that is fun to do is to have summer cookouts during the work week day. It seems that each staff has a "grill master" on board, who likes to show off his home brewed skills on the gas grill. Give him or her that opportunity!

Buying either store prepared food, or having each one brings a dish from home, helps create an "at ease" break during the work day. And it makes a good lunch too!

I know the Lord knew the importance of getting His team away from the daily routine, as He would take them apart from time to time. A time to be refreshed, to "recharge the batteries" is important in the business life as well. Just having time to stop doing the normal routine will help keep people desiring to give their best throughout the year.

Planning staff events ahead of time gives people the opportunity to look ahead, to anticipate the time out with the others. As we all like adventure and to get off the beaten path sometimes, give the staff these opportunities throughout the year.

Chapter 8

It Doesn't All Depend On You

There was a time, as I was nearing 30, that I told myself that I could do it all, that I really didn't need anyone to help me raise a family, take care of a house, fix the car, or need others to get a job done at the office. I soon found out that I was wrong!

Not only did I need the counsel of parents, friends, pastors and others who could and would speak into my life, but I needed staff members in order to get the right job done on time, and in good order. Above all, the Lord spoke to me on a very specific occasion, to let me know that I needed others. Certain things weren't going to get done only by me, and He didn't want it to be that way, anyway. I needed others.

During my service with a ministry, one of the staff I had with me decided to move back to Florida, from where he had come a few years earlier. Before that time, Bob Lafferty had become my right hand man, very capable of doing things alongside me, with us working very well together. I depended on him for much.

I had a choice to make – to hire another to take his place, or go back and do those things which I had done myself before he had come on staff to help. In order to save the ministry money, with less payroll costs, I was going to take the road I normally took, which was to try and do it all myself. I was going to continue on without another in that place, saving money, but burning myself out in the process.

If ever I heard the voice of the Lord, it sure was then! As I walked to the back room of the converted home-to-office setup, to prepare another product order for shipment, I clearly heard the Lord speak to my spirit. "If you go backwards, you will never go forwards." I knew exactly what He was talking about!

He certainly was telling me, that as the administrator, it was my place to hire another person, take the time to train them, and continue on doing what I was gifted and given to do. If I chose to not hire someone, I would be stuck doing those tasks that others could be doing, and should be doing. That would have kept me from not only doing what I was supposed to be doing, and should be doing, but I would be the one to pay the price in personal wear and tear in my life, and of those around me.

As with any part of the body, both in the natural body and the church spiritually body, we each have specific parts of the body that were created to do certain functions. If each part isn't doing its intended function, the whole body has to compensate, resulting in disorder or more strain on the body.

For example, if a hand tries to compensate for a foot that isn't there, or the foot is not able to function properly, then the hand is prevented from doing its proper role, as it tries to "replace" the foot by doing the foot's role. In all practically it simply can't. The body will end up moving in an awkward way, trying to compensate for the part that is lacking, or isn't capable of doing.

And so I obeyed the Lord and hired a replacement. After taking the extra time to train him, even though in the short run it took more time, in the long run he filled the hole very well, and I was able to continue doing the responsibilities that I needed, and only could, do. The new man did the shipping and mail runs while I did the accounting and the purchasing. Each of us was doing our part. The church was built up and strengthened because he was there to do his job, and I was again able to do mine. The Lord blessed us both in the work.

As the workload of the office expanded, I needed to know when to hire on, and when to have the current staff press a bit more, to do the extra required during the current period of increase. I also had to hear the voice of the Lord and others who could bring advice as needed. Are the tasks at hand to be done a short time task, or would this build into something for the long term? Did we hire for part-time, fulltime, or contract services? What are the costs of the additional benefits going to cost, for medical insurance, vacation and sick time, and paid holidays? These are ongoing questions that the administrator has to answer on a regular basis quite often.

Different criteria have helped me when making this decision. I consider the annual costs the new staff addition would be, and weigh that against the benefit they will add to the growth of the office. If the current staff is working at full production level, and no one else can be asked to work longer hours, then the need presses itself to be taken care of sooner rather than later. If another project or outreach is added to the overall work of the office, then certainly another staff member would be the reasonable answer to bring the desires of the leadership to fruition.

Another consideration needing to be reviewed is whether this is a direct income-producing job, or if the additional staff will encourage income to come in as a result of the tasks they perform. A new assistant on the phones won't outright increase funds, but their taking a load off another, who then can produce more written work or phone calling, will add to the overall bottom line. The stress level of the entire staff is also kept at a reasonable level.

As you slowly build your staff, growing as the church, ministry or business increases, this gives new employees the opportunity to add their talents to the crew. The administrator becomes more of a "quarterback", directing the flow of paperwork, production levels, and advancement, rather than doing the tasks that others can and should do.

What then depends on you is to keep seeking the Holy Spirit, to hear His voice, and trust in His guidance day by day. As things do flow and ebb, the administrator needs to know when to push in some areas, back off in others, and keeps the staff alert to the ongoing overall work needing to be accomplished. During the slower or seasonal times, tasks to prepare for the upcoming busy season need to be done in advance. The good administrator will keep his eyes looking forward to the days ahead, planning today what needs to happen tomorrow, rather than just waiting for fires to be put out or until the "push to deliver" gets too strong.

As you grow, you need to be looking for those who have the gifting and desire to become leaders on the team, who can learn more directly from you. As you yourself grow in responsibilities and commitments, you will need those who can give direction and guidance in areas that you release them into that you formerly covered. Do not fear giving responsibility, and also the authority, to others, to get jobs done. If you were to continue to believe that only you can do it, the day will come when the tasks assigned to your control have grown too big, and too overwhelming, and by then you better have others in place to take on some of your former tasks.

I have seen those in administrative positions who fear giving someone part of their work, lacking trust, or going on past experiences when they have passed on work. As administrators, we need to entrust to others responsibilities, or else the work is bottlenecked with us, which slows, or stops, the work flow of others.

It does not all depend on us. If we are faithful to work diligently, the work will grow, and others will be added to do the work alongside us. We need to be willing and trusting to let others be added, take on tasks that we did well, and actually excel beyond what we had taken the previous level to.

Insecurity is one area we need to be aware of, which can keep us from allowing others to succeed. There have been times when I have seen leaders keep things in their control, not wanting to release responsibilities, with authority, due to their own insecurities. Being jealous of a subordinate for certain gifts that they excel at, while holding onto their territory, has many times kept leaders from allowing the ministry or business to grow.

If we allow the Lord to give us His security in our areas of expertise, and acknowledge that others have areas that they will excel in, then we are free to give room for others to grow, and even surpass the work we could have done.

One area that I particularly liked building was setting up book tables, establishing book stores or gift shops with the three ministries I have worked for. I felt I had a good way of laying out the tables, arranging the product, and having good traffic flow for the crowd. I prided myself on how well I felt I did this, and appreciated hearing the good comments from staff and customers.

In time, as others came on staff, and I listened to their ideas regarding the layouts, I found they could do it just as well as I could. In order to let them "take ownership" also, I needed to step out of the way and let them. I knew it was time to "pass the baton", to see them grow in their gifting and skill level. It was important for me to release this area I did well in, into the hands of others who came behind me.

I also knew that they would have different ideas and methods than I did or would, and I needed to give them the room to try these out. I could add my thoughts, but I needed to give them plenty of room to do their thing.

As I did this, in this area and in others, new leadership was raised up, and new doors were then opened to me. I was secure in the Lord to pass this responsibility on, knowing that He could entrust other works into my hands. If I had held onto this "cup", I wouldn't have received the next larger one He had in store for me.

Leadership is raised up as the current leaders give those coming behind them room to make mistakes, and take control over time. This keeps progress advancing, and growth is apparent as new ideas and procedures are put in place.

Chapter 9

Practically Speaking…and Walking

- Handle each piece of paper once
- File so you can find it!
- Early morning – before the others come
- Take a Break

Every job has some tools that can be applied, and some guidelines and methods that help do a good work. Over the 40 years of management with businesses and ministries, there are some helpful methods that have worked for me, and which I'd like to pass onto you.

From time to time I felt it helpful to attend "day seminars", to learn any possible new thing. One that proved to be very beneficial, and made it worth the $99 paid back in the early '80's, was this: handle a piece of paper once.

How many stacks of paper do you currently have on your desk? How many file folders do you have, in the two-drawer or four-drawer filing cabinets? How many times have you picked up the same irritating piece of paper, that you just didn't want to deal with, and then put it back in the stack to pick it up again the next hour, or the next day or week?

After one seminar, where the spokesman had given a list of helpful, daily "To DO" items, one I actually tried to master was this: handle a piece of paper once.

I had heard that it takes 90 days to learn a regular discipline, and so I tried this one, determined to "pay for" that $99 investment.
Beginning the next day at the office, I picked up a piece of paper that had been sitting on my desk, and I did one of several things:

(1) I marked the date I received it, with my initials.
(2) I wrote what action I was going to take with it – file, call, or write a response.
(3) I did what I wrote I was going to do – I made the call, wrote the response, and filed it in a paper folder for the file cabinet.

If I needed to retrieve it later, I knew what file folder I had placed it in, and I didn't have to look through the stack of papers still on my desk, in several piles.

As I went through my stacks, I did the same thing – mark date received, action taken, file away for later retrieval as needed. My stacks began to shrink in size, and the daily pressure I had often previously, when I arrived at my desk and looked at the stacks, lessened.

In association with this, I am big on filing. But not only to file, but to know where you filed it in order to get it, when you need it. It doesn't do a whole lot of good to file documents away and then not be able to retrieve them. It is critical that the hanging file folders, and the computer data folders, are labeled in such a way that you know under what label you put it.

On several occasions, there may be several choices under which to file a certain piece of information. In this case, I learned to think which category would I first think it would make sense to file it under, and so I did. Just as a library has more than one listing for a different book, you may also need to do this, just in case you forget which file you used.

When you have someone process your daily mail, I have found it most helpful to use two colored file folders. One is marked "Priority Mail" (I like a green folder for this) and the other, of another color, is marked "Misc. Mail". The personal letters, cards, and invoices from vendors go into this folder, while advertising, appeal letters, and such are put in the other folder. Magazines and catalogs are not placed in either folder. I can view them quickly, placing half immediately in the garbage can, along with the other junk mail.

When you have time to only look through some of the mail, it is the green "Priority Mail" folder that you will know to grab first.

Every administrator knows that interruptions are a daily occurrence, and that we just need to expect them. No matter how well you set up appointments, schedule daily or weekly tasks, or arrange meetings to administrate upcoming events, there are always interruptions that seem to take preference over anything else.

To offset ongoing, daily "fires" that needed putting out, I began coming into the office at least an hour before the other staff members. Just having that extra hour gave me needed time to get my day in order as best I could, or to complete a task that didn't get done the day before. As much as you can, as the administrator of the business or ministry you work with, try to book these times where you know that it would be a major event to get you away from this "quiet, get it done" time. Even make it known to others ahead of time, that unless the church is burning down, you need uninterrupted time to yourself. For me, this is first thing in the morning.

During the day, take breaks too! If much of your work is performed at the desk on the computer, then you need to take breaks by just getting up, walking to greet the others, or see how things are going on in other locations other than your room. Just moving from one spot to another can clear your head, give you a chance to think about other things, or simply to stretch. Too much concentration on one subject in one sitting made me too weary to give it what I needed. A short break helped the blood flow a bit better, to get back to the task at hand.

Chapter 10

Meetings – Time Manger or Time Waster?

- Do you really need all those meetings?
- Group or One-On-One?
- Why morning and mid-week?
- Prov. 24:6 "By wise counsel…multitude of counselors

As the CEO, director, administrator, office manager, administrative assistant, or leader of any size group, have you ever thought of how many hours you have spent in administrative meetings with more than two people? I am sure I have spent more time in meetings than was really necessary.

There are some leaders who just love meetings. They met to discuss the day, the week, the month, the year, and then meet next week to do the same thing. Seems at times that there is more "talk" than "walk", as meetings consume our time. Though we think we are wisely planning, we may in reality be wasting each other's time.

I am not a "meeting" person. (Bet you couldn't tell!) When given the option of meeting in a larger group, I have more often chosen to communicate one on one than having a group sit around a rectangular board room table talk about things that were talked about last time, and nothing much has happened in between.

Being one who enjoys history, and reading of leaders and their habits, it seems to me that the "modern" executive or leader in the office setting has swung the pendulum too far to the "MEETING" side in communicating. Of course we don't have all the minutes and details of communications from ages gone by, but I would have to think that more was done "outside of the meeting room" than what occurred within.

Meetings do have a purpose. When discussions need to involve more than two people, due to the responsibilities of each, then of course meetings are necessary. There are certain criteria that I have followed which has helped me in having a good meeting when it was needed.

The first criteria I have had in place is to set the beginning and the ending time of the meeting, so there is no needless dragging on and endless talk, leading nowhere. If you schedule people more than an hour for a meeting, you can almost be assured that they will let the time fill up as allowed.

Most meetings can be accomplished in a half hour. The one calling the meeting needs to have some discussion topics sent to each one coming to the meeting ahead of time. Then each one can gather their thoughts and give them at the appropriate time. Time allowed for discussion between individuals needs to be included in the meeting timeline.

As people become accustomed to the shorter time frame, the dialogue is kept on topic and thus unnecessary talk is limited. With each knowing ahead of time what will be covered, they had time prior to the gathering to formulate their input, rather than attempting to do it during the time together.

Morning meetings are more preferred than the afternoon time. Especially avoid the time right after lunch. People's minds are more alert in the mid-morning time than the mid-afternoon. And do you know one of the rather unexpected results of shorter, morning meetings? Drowsiness is curtailed to a minimum! (I had been known to "dream prophetic dreams" during long, boring meetings, especially in the afternoon!)

I also believe that a mid-week meeting is more productive than certainly a Monday or Friday meeting. Weekends, meant to be a "break" for most workers, has now become two of the most busy days in the lives of the typical worker, and thus the weekend off is taking more of a toll on people. No Sabbath time for the typical worker these days is taking its predicted cost. Even many Christians, and especially the administrators and assistants in the church positions, are especially taxed over the weekend, with the one Sunday, and often two, church meetings, and other church gatherings that typically take place on the Saturday or Sunday day off.

One on one times with individual staff members not only gets more accomplished with the quality time, but the staff member has more of an opportunity to share their real thoughts, desires, and feedback more honestly. Without the pressure of having to, or wanting to, impress co-workers in a group meeting, they can express their thoughts and feelings more directly to their supervisor. It also prevents the one or two dominant personalities from overtaking a meeting.

Proverbs 24:6 states "By wise counsel…in the multitude of counselors." I apply this verse not only in my spiritual life, but also in the business of ministry. Surrounding yourself with good staff, which have different gifts and skills than what you as the leader has, not only makes good business sense, but also lets you hear the mind of the Lord when needing to make those every day, and also critical, decisions.

Chapter 11

Acknowledge Him in All Your Ways

- Heart of Thankfulness
- Heart of Worship
- Heart of Service

The very first verse I ever memorized that I can remember was Psalm 37:4, 5 "Have your delight in the Lord, and He will give you the desire of your heart. Trust also in Him, and He will do it." (NAS) That was in my teen years, before the "work" years began.

After twenty years of administration work, I can truthfully and gratefully acknowledge that if it hadn't been for the Lord's encouragement, guidance, provision, patience and persistence working in my life through His grace, I would have quit ministry service a long time ago. Administrative staff serving in key roles need to depend on Him in all that they set out to do. The road is not easy, and our spirits, souls and bodies need His constant input to refresh, revitalize, and direct our daily steps.

Ministry and church administration, though it has the eternal rewards promised to all faithful servants, is certainly not the "field of green" that many expect it is. As in any work of the Lord, there are additional pressures that one confronts knowingly and unknowingly throughout the week. The enemy of the soul seems to work overtime to discourage, steal and destroy the families and staff of committed laborers. Those at the "top of the staff rosters" are generally the first target.

Having raised a family of four with my wife Laurie, we have experienced the results of the enemy's efforts to get us off course. Often he will work through our children, to try and have us question the protection and watch care the Lord promises.

Having had four cars totaled in the early driving years of our three oldest kids certainly tested our faith. The three trips to bail two out of jail on separate other occasions, even more so caused us to seek the Lord for His wisdom and counsel. Our home lives do have the spiritual pressure bearing down on us, as we attempt to set the examples of leadership in the church and ministry settings.

To acknowledge the ongoing reliance on the Lord's protection and provision are continually needed to press forward, to see His kingdom come and His will done. One prophetic word spoken over me that I didn't realize until I heard it only recently, was that the Lord has His protection over and around me. One may take that for granted, which I did, but when it came through my ears and settled into my heart, my gratitude for the Lord increased. That spoken word continues to give me the faith to push forward in those areas of building and growth that I have been called to do. Knowing my back and forward progress is protected gives me the courage to press on, which also includes my family.

To help sustain this awareness of the Lord's presence, it has become my habit to spend the quiet time each day with the Lord, as I wrote in an earlier chapter. I need to thank my mother for her excellent example set early in my childhood. As a kid growing up in Cedar Falls, Iowa, I noticed her take time out at the beginning of the day to read the Word, listen to her praise albums on the stereo phonograph player, and pray. To this day, this practice in my life has been ongoing (except on Saturdays and Sundays, when I commit my day to the Lord in others ways.)

Developing a thankful heart as a leader, by thanking the Lord for the opportunities He gives in service as a leader, allows me to realize just what all He does. When a situation arises that could cause grave concern or another headache, my first reaction has often been to say quietly to the Lord, "Thank you Lord." To speak blessing instead of cursing, when the temptation is great to do otherwise in any situation, causes the matter to be handled with a more godly response.

When I lay my head down to sleep, as it hits the pillow, I have made it a habit to simply say "Thank you Lord."

Leading worship in church has been one of my greatest joys. A favorite songs is one by Don Moen (Integrity Music) entitled "*Thank You Lord*". When I would lead that song at the beginning of a praise and worship service, the atmosphere is charged with people's hearts giving thanks to the Lord right from the start. Cares and concerns seem to diminish as each acknowledges his dependence on the goodness of the Lord, and thanking Him for his blessings.

Being an avid reader, I have found time spent reading books on the faith of saints who have preceded us builds a thankful heart in me. That in turn assists me in encouraging others on staff in their faith, by them seeing and hearing of my thankful heart.

I remember one situation in the office that certainly needed a spoken word of thanks, so that something else would not have come forth. It seems that in the building we had purchased a few years early, when the back parking lot was laid, the sewer line was not given the proper degree of angle needed for outward flow. Over the years, as the weight of the earth above it shifted and sunk, it put pressure on the line at one end, causing the line to push up at the wrong end. Thus the water flow ceased flowing. At least in the right direction!

When the backed up mess ended up in two lower level offices, you can imagine the consternation that ensued. If the Lord hadn't developed a thankful heart in me, I would have reacted as one would have expected, along with the occupants of those rooms. But instead, I was able to track down a plumber to start the proper course of action, and in the meantime, got out the wet vac and started doing the necessity work. No fun for sure, but at least I wasn't grumbling to high heaven.

Another time, at a previous administrator position, a swimming pool that came with the leased property had to have the annual cleaning after winter was over. Having grown up going to the pool three times a day in my young grade school years, I had grown basically tired of swimming and water, and anything related to it. This brought me no joy. And then especially when the pool covering had fallen half in, during the eight months of not doing its job. Of course, every tree leaf, twig, dead mice and other creatures that couldn't swim found their way to this part of the property.

After sucking out the totally polluted water, and shoveling out the extra-terrestrial creatures and creation as listed above, hours later I was able to give some thanks. The job was over! Through tasks like this, by doing things we normally detest, our hearts are given the opportunity to serve others, and develop thankfulness. It also helps us to grow in further appreciation for those who the Lord surrounds us with who help us in times a need, who do tasks and chores that aren't at all pleasant, but need to get done.

Art Maki, a longtime friend of over 20 years, has most often been that special one in our lives, and the church he blessed daily with his service. As Art will say every time one is with him, "Jesus loves you, and so do the Makis", to remind each of the Lord's love and care, for which we owe much thanks. Thank you Art!

Chapter 12

Another Man's Vineyard
(...and now my own.)

-Follow & help fulfill their vision
-Faithful with another's
-Learn and growth until your time
-The proper way of moving on

For close to 24 years I served as the Administrator or Director of Operations & Finance for three different ministries, doing that which I knew to do. Together with the leaders of those respective ministries, we laid foundations and established further the "vineyard" that the Lord had entrusted to the founders.

As a vital part of the work, being faithful in adding to the building and the ongoing structure did enable me to do my part in seeing the work of the Lord done. The Lord was glorified, people were "built up" in the faith, buildings were restored and placed into the work of the kingdom, and the vineyard produced lasting fruit.

My heart was given to the Lord through these ministries, but as time passed, there were things the Lord had been calling me to do, which my heart's cry was to see them fulfilled. Beginning with what He had instilled in me, even as a young child, to be a missionary and take the gospel to the nations, and with ongoing prophetic words, the desire to have my own vineyard grew evermore present.

My natural gifts, which are an expression of the spiritual gifts He had given me, were in administration, accounting and general management of inventories, staff and daily tasks, but my heart so longed to "not sit behind a desk 40 hours a week", but to travel and take His love beyond the local setting. Often I expressed that desire to those I was under, and to fellow workers. At times the desire was so intense, and I repeatedly asked the Lord when I would be delivered from the desk job to something that I knew for me was more.

During this time, the ongoing struggle to be faithful with the daily tasks, while at the same time praying and yearning for the adventurous tasks, was very difficult. Trying to keep focused on the maintenance of the ministry, when I wanted so much to be in the movement of the ministry reminded me of Joseph in prison. He was in the Lord's will I am sure, and yet the constant waiting of when that time would be over and he would be out of prison was something I could very much relate to.

At times I was even resentful of those who had the opportunities to go, while I stayed and manned the fort. When I would hear them speak of the strain of travel and that type of ministry, but silent response was, "Then you stay and let me go instead", but it never happened. I didn't want to have the inner struggle of believing the grass is greener on the other side, but I honestly longed for the opportunities to travel in ministry.

Even more discouraging during the years when I was the administrator of one ministry where the leaders were often traveling, people would ask me if I went along to the distant lands and people, and I had to respond "No." It was hard to continue convincing myself that this was the place the Lord had for me, and I needed to be fulfilled in doing what I had been given to do. My job was to take care of the office and staff, while it was their job to "go".

After many years of this struggle, I finally had to do something, and so asked if I could at least once go on an international trip with them. When the response came back as no, then to keep my having the ache of the heart continue, I gave my resignation notice, and began looking for the next position I believed the Lord would give me.

So what do you do as the administrator, or key person in an organization, and though you are good at what you are doing, your heart just is no longer in it? For me, I knew I had to move on, or else my heart and attitude would have become very bitter, and I would have brought harm to the organization, rather than being a constructive part of the work.

When you are faced with this decision, the Lord does give you the proper way to leave a situation. In the times when I have left two business and three ministry positions, He has generally given me a year's notice prior to the course change up ahead. In my desire to then bless those whom I was leaving, I gave a three to six month notice, in order for them to find the right replacement and have training done for my position.

Even when I didn't have another position lined up, the Lord honored my commitment I had with current leadership, to not leave them in a precarious place in their own work. And for each of these five job changes, He had brought a good replacement for the work, and also led me to the next place that I was needed at.

There is always a proper way to leave one situation for another. As hard as change can be, and yet necessary, the Lord will reveal His plan if asked, and if each party is open to listening. I am thankful that that has happened in each case for me. I believe my honesty and faithfulness throughout the years I was on each job was a key factor in how the leadership blessed me in my leaving, and how I had blessed them.

During the transition time, the company or ministry had time to find another person to take my place. On three occasions I was able to recommend an assistant whom I had trained properly, and so the transition went very smooth. On two other occasions I recommended known friends who had the skills to take over as I was leaving. They were hired, based on my recommendation.

I in turn had time to prepare my family, and to search for the next location of employment. Knowing that indeed it is true, "For I know the plans I have for you, says the Lord, plans for welfare and not for calamity", gave me confidence that I was hearing the Lord during this transition, and that He was going to direct my steps. Even when I didn't have a position in place at the time of my resignation notices, my faith in the Lord's provision was constant. He had proven Himself trustworthy to me, and thus I was able to put my trust in Him.

As Derek Prince often said, "He is Faithful." He certainly is!

And Now My Own

On November 23, 2009, my 55th birthday, I gave my resignation notice to the president and founder of Vision for Israel, the third ministry I had then served with for five years. Having based this decision on several factors, beginning with the Lord's desires that He had put in my heart (some since I was ten years of age); prophetic words received over many years, which brought encouragement and built up my faith; and knowing the time was now right to step out and start my "own vineyard", I myself became the founder of **Love For His People, Inc**. With other believers, we bless believers in Israel, India, Africa, the USA, and other nations.

I am both excited and full of faith, mindful that my trust rests on solid ground - the Lord Jesus Christ Himself.

As a final thought, keep your eyes fixed on the Lord in all situations, and you will see Him direct your steps into His full purposes for you. I for one can testify of His faithfulness and His provision in all.

Carry on!

Steve Martin

ABOUT THE AUTHOR

Steve Martin served with three Christian ministries from 1987-2010, all having a national and international outreach focus. During that time he made 14 ministry trips to Israel, China, India, Trinidad and Tobago, and the United Kingdom.

On his overseas journeys Steve enjoyed sharing written journal entries with family and friends back home, through Internet media. His light-hearted stories gave an up close and personal touch for those reading along. Many could imagine being there themselves.

His extensive collection of photos taken during these trips, of both local scenery and common people on the streets, has touched thousands through their varied images.

In 2010, Steve and Laurie began "Love For His People, Inc," a 501©3 non-profit humanitarian aid ministry. This work touches the natural and spiritual lives of those around them with needed encouragement and strength.

His regular "Ahava Love Letter", posted both on the *Love For His People* Blog and Facebook, feature his love letters of spiritual enrichment, plus selected photos and commentary from abroad.

Since 1994, Steve and his good wife Laurie have lived in the Charlotte, NC area, after having homes in Illinois, Michigan and

Florida. Now married for more than 36 years, they enjoy their four adult children and spouses, along with six additional grandchildren.

While continuing to serve organizations with his accounting skills, he enjoys writing and growing the ministry of Love For His People, Inc.

CONTACT INFORMATION

I hope you enjoyed my book. Please share with me some of your life's journey.

You can also get my books, ***The Promise*** (CreateSpace/Martin Lighthouse Publishing, 2013*)*, and ***Ahava Love Letters*** (Xulon Press, 2013) on website book stores and though our ministry.

Contact me in the following ways:

Steve Martin
Love For His People, Inc.
P.O. Box 414
Pineville, NC 28134 USA

Email: loveforhispeople@gmail.com
martinlighthouse@gmail.com

Facebook pages: *Steve Martin* and *Love For His People*

Twitter: *martinlighthous, LovingHisPeople, LoveHisPeople* and *ahavaloveletters*

Blogger: http://loveforhispeople.blogspot.com

YouTube: Steve Martin (loveforhispeopleinc)

Website: www.loveforhispeople.org

Our Love For His People, Inc. ministry is a USA Non-profit 501(c)3. Fed. ID #27-1633858.

We welcome your gifts and communications of support, as we continue to provide humanitarian aid to our Israel, India and African connections. We hope you will become connected too along with us, and send a one-time gift or become a regular, monthly friend. Thank you very much for this consideration!

You can send checks, or contribute through our PayPal account on our website: http://www.loveforhispeople.org/support.html
With this I close, as I do with all my *Ahava Love Letters*,

Ahava (*love* in Hebrew) to my family of friends,

Steve Martin
Founder/President
Love For His People, Inc.

P.S. We send tax deductible receipts for all gifts received for the work of the ministry!

Also available on Amazon.com and from our ministry office.

The Promise (2013)

Ahava Love Letters (2013)

Steve's *Ahava Love Letters*, written weekly, can be found on **www.loveforhispeople.blogspot.com and www.ahavaloveletters.blogspot website.**

Our ministry website, **www.loveforhispeople.org,** features regular articles of interest and our ministry updates.

www.ingramcontent.com/pod-product-compliance
Lightning Source LLC
Chambersburg PA
CBHW071809170526
45167CB00003B/1230